That Quote!

journal belongs to...

© 2017 Ranch House Press
All rights reserved. Printed in the United States of America.

www.annettebridges.com

ISBN: 978-1-946371-18-8

Journal Prompts
That Quote!

Use this journal to collect quotes that speak to your soul in some way. Here are some quotes to get you thinking. For these quotes and the ones you add, ask yourself these questions: What does this quote mean to me? How does it apply to my life?

1. We act as though comfort and luxury were the chief requirements of life, when all that we need to make us happy is something to be enthusiastic about. ~ Einstein
2. It takes no more time to see the good side of life than it takes to see the bad. ~ Jimmy Buffet
3. Remember, happiness doesn't depend upon who you are or what you have; it depends solely on what you think. ~ Dale Carnegie
4. May you live all the days of your life. ~ Unknown
5. It's not the mountain we conquer, but ourselves. ~ Sir Edmund Hillary
6. Curiosity is one of the permanent and certain characteristics of a vigorous mind. ~ Unknown
7. Millions say the apple fell, but Newton was the one to ask why. ~ Bernard M. Baruch
8. When I look back on all these worries I remember the story of the old man who said on his deathbed that he had had a lot of trouble in his life, most of which never happened. ~ Winston Churchill
9. The greater danger for most of us is not that our aim is too high and we miss it, but that it is too low and we reach it. ~ Michelangelo Buonarroti
10. Learn to be silent. Let your quiet mind listen and absorb. ~ Pythagoras
11. Most folks are about as happy as they make their minds to be. ~ Abe Lincoln
12. A good traveler has no fixed plans and is not intent on arriving. ~ Lao Tzu
13. Sometimes you will never know the value of a moment until it becomes a memory. ~ Dr. Seuss
14. Write what should not be forgotten. ~ Isabel Allende
15. The act of writing is the act of discovering what you believe. ~ David Hare
16. Fill your paper with the breathings of your heart. ~ William Wordsworth
17. Start where you are. Use what you have. Do what you can. ~ Arther Ashe
18. The only person you are destined to become is the person you decide to be. ~ Ralph Waldo Emerson
19. Our greatest weakness lies in giving up. The most certain way to succeed is always to try just one more time. ~ Thomas Edison
20. Even if you fall on your face, you're still moving forward. ~ Victor Kiam
21. You must do the things you think you cannot do. ~ Eleanor Roosevelt
22. Be not afraid of life. Believe that life is worth living, and your belief will help create the fact. ~ William James
23. When I let go of what I am, I become what I might be. ~ Lao Tzu
24. You may find the worst enemy or best friend in yourself. ~ English Proverb
25. Whoever loves much, performs much, and can accomplish much, and what is done in love is done well. ~ Vincent Van Gogh
26. The great thing in this world is not so much where you stand, as in what direction you are moving. ~ Oliver Wendell Holmes
27. Live each day as if your life had just begun. ~ Johann Wolfgang Von Goethe
28. Either you run the day, or the day runs you. ~ Jim Rohn
29. If not us, who? If not now, when? ~ John F. Kennedy
30. Don't worry about failures, worry about the chances you miss when you don't even try. ~ Jack Canfield

color your world

ABOUT the CREATOR

Annette Bridges is an author, publisher and women's retreat host on a mission to help every woman realize her story is extraordinary, valuable and noteworthy.

She has published the *Color Your World Journal Series* and formed a journal club to provide community, support and tools for women to record their ideas, feelings, experiences, memories and all the important details of their lives.

Before writing books and publishing journals and coloring books, this former public school and homeschool educator spent a decade writing hundreds of helpful, instructive, and light-hearted columns published by Texas newspapers, parenting magazines, websites and bloggers.

Annette lives on a Texas cattle ranch with her husband John, dachshund Lady and lots of cows. She can drive a tractor but only if wearing a fresh coat of lipstick and it's not her pedicure day!

You can learn more about Annette's books and products, blogs and videos as well as her women's retreats and other events at www.annettebridges.com.

Look for her on social media, too!

Message from the Publisher

The ***Color Your World Journal Series*** is a pathway to self-discovery. It's where you write notes to yourself. Be your own cheerleader. Give yourself encouragement. Tell yourself what you're grateful for. Celebrate you!

There are countless reasons to keep a journal including collecting favorite recipes, listing goals and celebrating every experience and every one that's near and dear to you. A journal provides a home for the memories and lessons learned that you never want to forget.

Why a niche journal?

If you're anything like me, you have a journal (or even two or three journals) where you write anything and everything about anything and everything. My challenge comes when trying to find something I've written. I flip and flip through the pages of my two, three or four journals trying to find whatever it is. I never remember which journal I wrote down my whatever's!!

The solution? A niche journal! A journal that has a specific focus and theme! A journal where you can record your ideas, inspirations and things you want to remember in the appropriate journal.

Why big unlined paper?

Because big unlined paper is needed to record big ideas, dreams and memories! You need room to grow, stretch and expand. You need space to think beyond the confines of what you've always done, to pursue new dreams, discover your power and reimagine your purpose again and again. You need pages without lines and limitations to reconnect with your creative, perfectly imperfect self.

Plus, big unlined paper gives you space for more than words. You have plenty of room to doodle, draw or post photographs and clippings, too.

Why color is important?

When you journal, use colored pens and markers! Your world doesn't happen in black and white. Your life should be lived and written about in many colors. Even dark and sad memories feel lighter and brighter when told in color.

Journaling in color affects your mood and perception of your world. Colors evoke calm, cheer and comfort. Using color can lift your spirit and inspire your imagination. You may be surprised by all the beautiful benefits from adding more color into your life story.

When journaling, give yourself time to listen to your heart and reflect. Breathe in the moments. Feel. Be quiet. Let yourself be totally and thoroughly present with your thoughts. Let your heart transform you and teach you new insights. Open your mind to consider new ideas and possibilities. You may find that what your heart teaches will be life changing.